Over 100
SALT
DOUGH

To Luciano, Michele, Matteo

ACKNOWLEDGEMENTS
To Mariuccia Motta for working so hard with me;
to Sandra and Luigia Imoti for putting up with
me and my dough; to Lisa Benvenuti for her
invaluable assistance; to Rossana Mungai and the
editorial staff of Benissimo for their willingness
to help; to Cristina Sperandeo for believing in me
and my art.

Thank you for the material supplied by APA of
Bologna.

This edition published 1995 by Merehurst Limited, Ferry
House, 51-57 Lacy Road, Putney, London SW15 1PR

ISBN: 1 85391 582 3

A catalogue record for this book is available from the
British Library.

English text copyright © Merehurst Limited 1995
Translated by Juliet Haydock
Edited by Heather Dewhurst
Design and typesetting by Jervis Tuttell
Photographs by Alberto Bertoldi
Printed in Italy

Over 100
SALT
DOUGH
PROJECTS

ROSMUNDA IMOTI

MEREHURST

CONTENTS

GIFTS AND IDEAS FOR THE HOME....59

IDEAS FOR CELEBRATIONS....99

IDEAS FOR CHRISTMAS....113

IDEAS FOR EASTER....135

CHARACTERS....145

INTRODUCTION

I first came across dough modelling more than ten years ago in a French magazine. The basic recipe and a few examples were given on a double page spread. Although I now realize that those particular pieces were nothing very exceptional, at the time I was captivated. I thought it impossible to make such marvels out of such simple ingredients.

In those days, all my time was taken up by a full-time job and family commitments. So I cut out that article on dough modelling and put it away in a drawer for future reference, together with other assorted information on papier mâché, leaf collages and the secrets of Irish crochet-work.
Two years ago, I finally found a little extra time for myself and dug those two pages out of a drawer now stuffed full of ideas waiting for a rainy day. This marked the occasion when dough modelling became for me what can only be described as a grand passion.

I believe dough modelling appeals to me so much because it feels like play. The dough is so malleable, soft and clean that it makes me feel like a child again. It can be made out of readily-available, cheap, natural ingredients. The beauty is that the game never actually ends, one simply becomes more skilled. Even beginners can make simple items in a few hours. You may wish to send something extra with a gift, celebrate an anniversary or simply say thank you. A model is always better than a card or flowers because you have made it yourself.

Later on, you can tackle something more demanding; perhaps something to hang in the kitchen or the children's bedroom. Whatever you make will arouse the admiration of family and friends. The best thing of all is to give such models as a gift, particularly for Christmas, because bread has always been a symbol of abundance and prosperity and is therefore a good omen.
I have only one piece of advice for anyone who wishes to take up this fabulous hobby. It is important never to feel entirely satisfied with your achievements. Do not be too hard on yourself, but always be humble enough to accept that you can do better.

ABOUT BREAD

Bread is a staple food of European countries and has been important since ancient times. Every town and village has its own traditional bread shapes: loaves, sticks, buns or rolls This huge variety of shapes suggest that people throughout the ages have used malleable dough to create objects full of meaning, not intended solely for food.

Numerous historical references describe the use of "bread sculptures" for ceremonies linked to some of the most meaningful moments of human existence, such as birth, death and marriage. For example, bread figures found in Greece were originally offered to Demeter, goddess of fertility, while the ancient Romans offered bread to Ceres, goddess of the harvest.

Because it is central to the Christian sacrament, bread assumed particular importance during Medieval times. Even today, in central America, fertility symbols are still modelled out of dough for wedding parties, and bread sculptures are made for the cult of the dead. The tradition of making dough shapes has been passed down from generation to generation in eastern Europe and in certain Germanic countries. Although present-day society no longer recognizes much of the symbolic meaning in certain sculptures, the temptation to form an infinity of shapes out of bread dough still remains. Bread modelling can be a high form of art and interest in this "new" handicraft is growing even in Italy. Yet this hobby appeals not only to do-it-yourself enthusiasts. Its attraction lies in the fact that bread sculptures hark back to ancient ways of expressing life, love an prosperity.

Such forms therefore make a meaningful and much appreciated gift.

GETTING

STARTED

Materials

DIFFERENT FLOURS PRODUCE VARYING RESULTS

Normal plain flour is ideal for making bread dough. It need not be particularly expensive, but the colour should be light and unflecked. Wholemeal flour or rye flour may also be used, either alone or mixed with white flour.

SALT

Try to use fine cooking salt. Excellent results may be achieved by grinding the salt in an old coffee mill until it is the consistency of icing sugar. One thing you will simply have to accept is that salt will eventually cause irretrievable damage to blades, cutters, scissors and any other small metal object used to carry out this handicraft.

Rye and whole-meal flour both produce a very dark, coarse dough. Dark doughs can be combined with ordinary white dough in large wreaths to produce interesting contrasting effects.

Remember that the dough produced by these flour types is not very malleable and can be difficult to knead.

OTHER ADDITIVES

Special additives may be added to the dough: powdered wallpaper paste, glycerine, edible oils, white vinegar, lemon juice or vinyl adhesives. Wallpaper paste will make the dough more malleable and give the finished item extra hardness. The modelled parts may also be assembled more easily without moistening. Add half a teaspoonful to the dry flour and salt mixture for every 10g (1/4oz) of flour. Glycerine and edible oils also make the dough softer and easier to knead. Both should be added to the dough in small quantities. Note that items containing oil tend to yellow with time. Vinegar and lemon juice make the finished item harder. A small amount of vinyl adhesive will help form a better dough and gives similar results to wallpaper paste. All these additives are absolutely optional and, to be honest, will never give miraculous results. Good results can only be obtained with experience.

Utensils

These are the essential working tools.

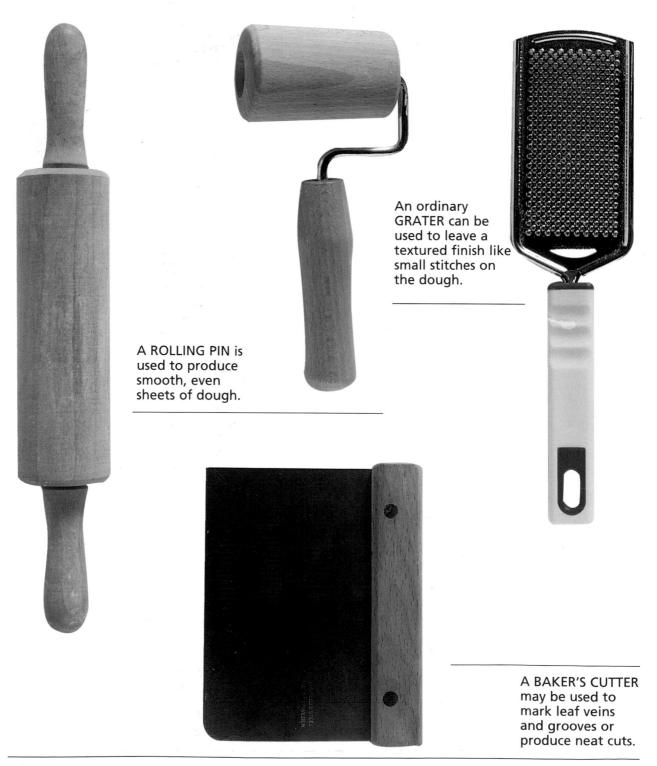

A ROLLING PIN is used to produce smooth, even sheets of dough.

An ordinary GRATER can be used to leave a textured finish like small stitches on the dough.

A BAKER'S CUTTER may be used to mark leaf veins and grooves or produce neat cuts.

PASTRY CUTTERS produce easy, foolproof results and can make life easier for beginners.

A wide selection of other small oddments can be found in any kitchen or home. Straws, unusual buttons, caps, lids, pen tops, combs, colanders, and other apparently uninteresting objects will make beautiful flower or star prints. A serendipitous joy is achieved when ordinary everyday objects can be put to unexpected new uses.

A GARLIC PRESS will produce long strands of dough, which can be used to make hair for your characters.

WOODEN TOOTH-PICKS, SKEWERS or **KEBAB STICKS** are useful for making holes.

Making salt dough for modelling

Mix the flour and salt (and the wallpaper paste, if used) in a large bowl. Add water at room temperature and knead vigorously to obtain a smooth, elastic dough. The procedure may also be carried out in reverse by dissolving the salt in water at room temperature and then adding flour. Another method involves using very hot water: dissolve the salt and then add the flour all at once. The resulting dough will be a little sticky, but the finished work will be very hard and tough. Extra water or salt may be added to any type of dough to obtain the necessary consistency and malleability. The longer the dough is kneaded, the better its appearance and malleability. The dough is also improved by being allowed to rest in a cool place for a few hours. Once prepared, the dough can be kept for up to a week if wrapped carefully in clingfilm and stored in a cool place (not the refrigerator). Although the dough will undoubtedly have become more moist when the wrapping is removed, this can be overcome by simply adding flour.

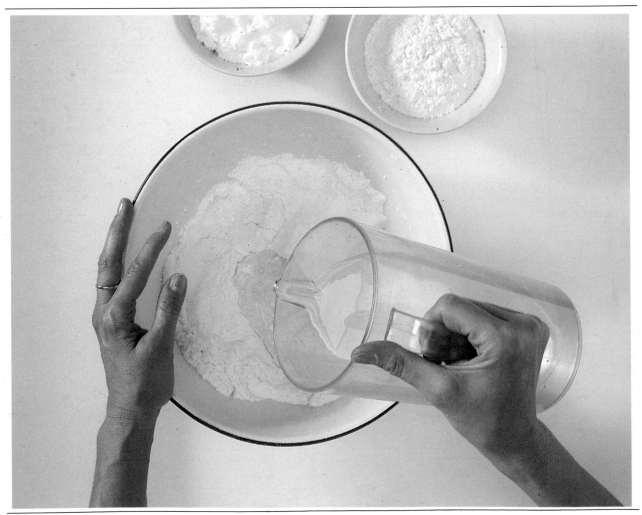

INGREDIENTS

200g (7oz) fine salt
200g (7oz) white flour
125ml (4fl oz) water

Or, without using scales:

1 cup fine salt
2 cups white flour
1 cup water

Note that minor changes in ingredient amounts will not affect the nature of the dough. Experience will teach you how to obtain the most effective results.

How to model

Before beginning work, prepare a small stock of colours wrapped in cling-film if you wish to use coloured dough. These can also be mixed together if required.

Keep all the tools you will require within easy reach: toothpicks, rolling pin, cutters and moulds. Do not forget a paint-brush and water.

Mould the various parts of your work individually and then put them together immediately by brushing with water and assembling gently. If forced to break off your work and resume later on, the joints between different parts will require extra moistening. It is advisable to work directly on a baking tray or a sheet of aluminium foil if the piece is to be baked. Remember to remove the foil as soon as possible as it prevents drying. Greaseproof paper is suitable for larger, thicker items, although small objects would be distorted by the ripples that form in the paper once dampened. Keep your hands and the working surface free of dry crumbs and colours. If the dough tends to dry or crack during use, simply knead with damp hands for a few minutes to restore elasticity. Conversely, use a little flour to dry the dough if it becomes too soft.

Baking and drying

Everyone who ever tries to make dough handicrafts eventually ruins one of their works by baking it incorrectly. Particular care and scrupulous temperature control is most important in the beginning when the dough is first put in the oven. Here too, no fixed rules or precise times can be given: everyone has their own methods and equipment, and of course their own idiosyncratic oven.

Long baking in a low oven (100°C/200°F/Gas Mark 1/4) is better, as a general rule, than short baking in a high oven, which could produce unexpected bubbles and unwelcome swelling. After an initial stage at a low heat the oven may be turned up to a medium heat. At the end, turn the oven up high enough to brown the piece nicely, but never exceed 180°C (350°F/Gas Mark 4). Shield parts of the piece with aluminium foil to achieve even browning or to brown one particular area more than another. Open the oven door every now and then during the drying process in order to allow part of the moisture to escape.

If you require a white end product or a light background for painting, the oven temperature should never exceed 100°C (200°F/Gas Mark 1/4) and the piece should be left in the oven until properly dried on top and underneath. Baking times may be reduced if the piece is firstly left in the open air for a period and then placed in the oven to complete the drying process. If the dough used for modelling has been coloured previously (particularly if pastel colours are used) try to avoid baking in an oven and dry in the open air or, if possible, on a radiator.

Decoration

COLOURED OR NATURAL

Certain models, such as large wreaths (instructions begin on page 60) are best left in the warm golden tones of natural bread. Other pieces also look fine in natural colours. For example, the angels on page 116 look as if they are made out of ivory.

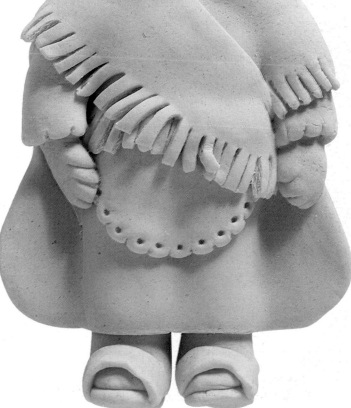

Other creations must be brightly coloured to catch the eye (see Hares and Country Cousins). Others, on the other hand, may only be executed in soft, delicate tones (see Dressers and Sweet boxes). You may decide to leave the piece as it is, colour the dough directly, or paint the finished item according to personal taste and skill.

Colouring the dough

To colour the dough, simply squeeze a little paint from a tube directly into white dough. Wear protective gloves and knead until the colour is even. Then wrap the coloured dough in clingfilm. The dough may then be used as it is or mixed with other coloured doughs to produce an infinite variety of shades. Finished items made out of coloured dough look neat and clean. They also form an excellent base for subsequent painted decoration applied using a brush.

Painting the finished item

It is very diffi-cult to paint onto a white base. Even experts risk unsightly paint runs. The colour may not always go on evenly but this method can be highly effec-tive if the paint is well applied.

Use paint in tubes and very fine brushes for small details.

Using fabrics for inspiration

Tiny sprigged muslins, or cottons with a fine stripe offer an inexhaustible fund of inspiration for effective decoration. It is advisable to begin with a dough in the same colour as the fabric background and then use a very fine brush to add the flowers in one colour before adding all the flowers in a second colour and a third and so on.

Another colour-ing technique uses very dilute colours, almost like washes, as in the case of this angel.

Watercolour effect

Adding decorative material

When the dough is still soft, material may be added (natural if possible) to create attractive effects. Dried flowers and wild grasses blend perfectly with natural and coloured items. Cloves, seeds, pepper-corns or small fruit stones may also be used. Note that items adorned in this way may not be baked in an oven but must be dried in the air. Exceptions are cloves and small seeds, which remain unaffected by heat. Small buttons, balls, feathers, beads, coloured stones or even pasta shapes may be used to add an extra touch to your creations. Experiment by all means, but do not get too carried away.

Adding gloss and finish

Pieces in very definite colours are much brighter and more attractive if treated with gloss varnish.

A matt varnish (spray-on is best) will improve the delicate appearance of a piece in muted colours.

Once complete, your piece requires protection against its only enemy: moisture. For this purpose it should be treated with a protective gloss or matt varnish. Excellent products of both types are available and the selection depends only on personal taste. The piece should be treated on the back as well and varnished only when perfectly dry.

Final tips

Remember to insert wire hooks or loops when the dough is still soft if you wish to hang your work. Open paper clips can also be used. Another quick way to hang your work is to make a hole on the back of the piece using a nail.

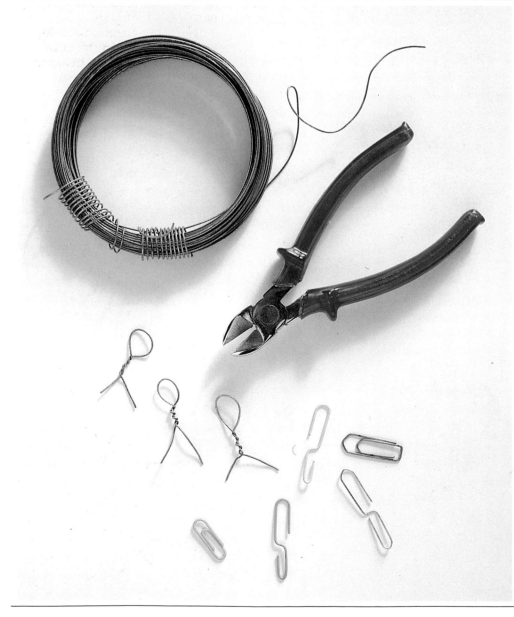

When giving a recently completed work as a gift, wrap the item in cellophane and tell the recipient to remove the wrapping and leave in the open for a while for better results. Keep a check on any masterpieces you have hung on the wall if you live in a damp place or experience a particularly rainy spell. It is advisable to stand items on a flat surface until the weather improves.

If one of your models breaks, try to repair it by putting fresh dough beneath the breakage point. Then smooth and mask the top with a moist finger before leaving the whole work to dry. Adhesive may also give excellent results, but in this case avoid re-hanging the repaired work.

Tricks of the trade

If you are in a hurry to complete a leaf and wish to obtain effective results, take any leaf with prominent veins (rose, mint or ivy will do), rest on the work surface and gently press a ball of dough on the leaf. Then simply taper the dough to a point and add serration if required for outstanding results.

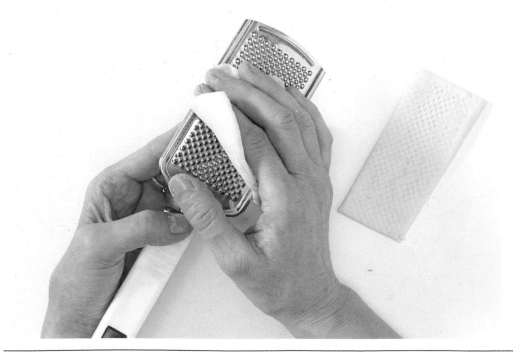

Use a small grater or textured lace to obtain the effect of embroidered fabric.

Achieve a basketwork effect by printing. Simply press the dough against a wicker basket.

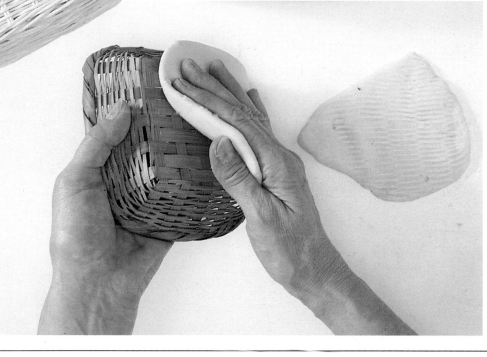

If you wish to make extremely fine, delicate petals for roses, simply press dough balls wrapped between two layers of clingfilm against the work surface.

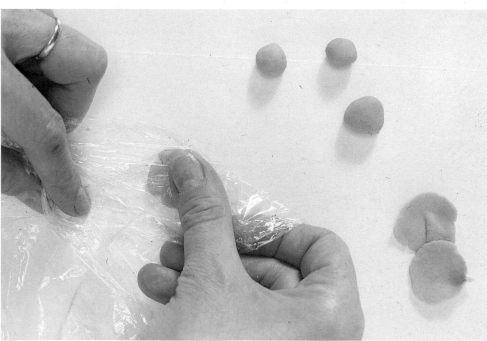

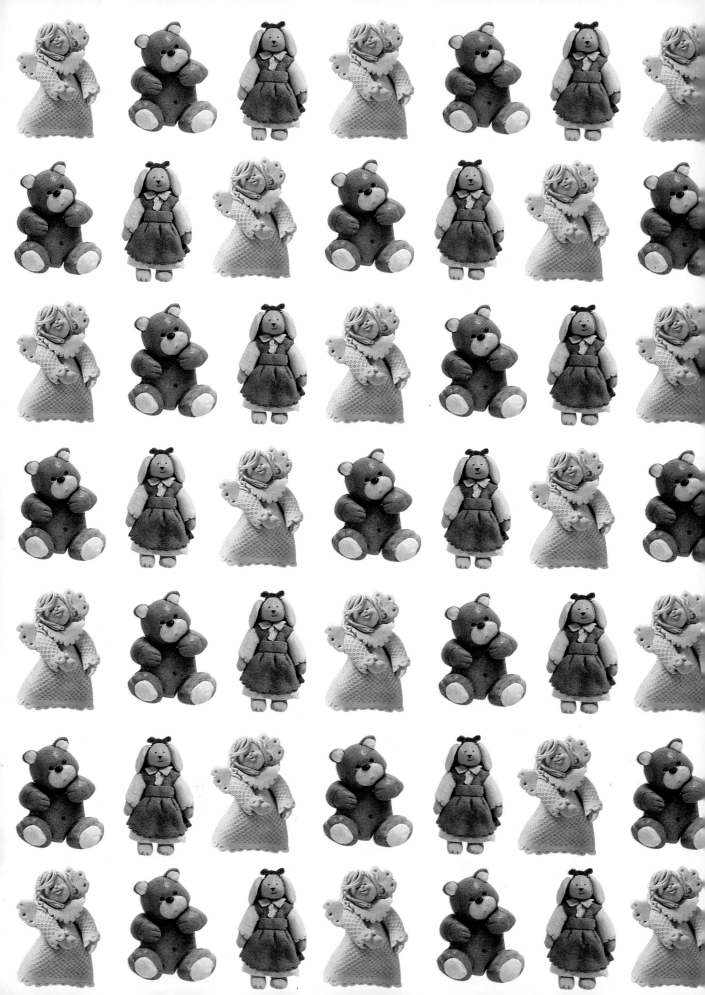

TECHNIQUES

Leaf

Note also the other method for creating an unfolded leaf illustrated on page 28.

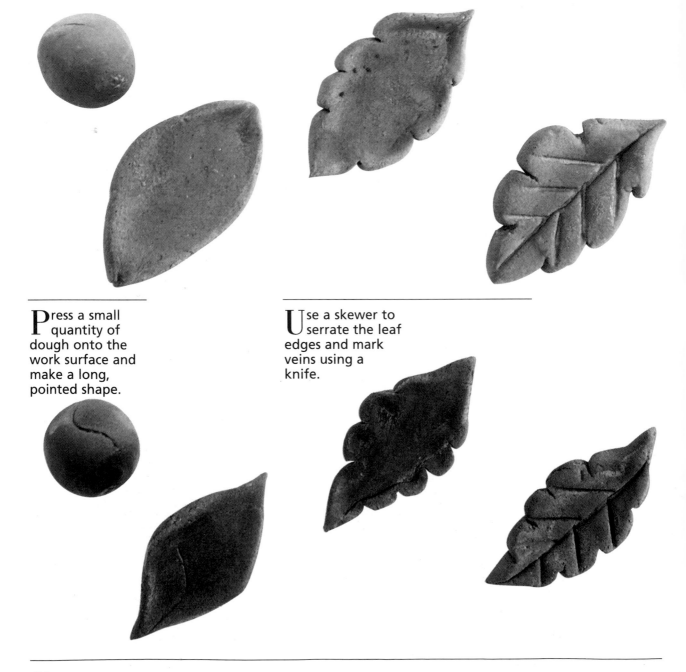

Press a small quantity of dough onto the work surface and make a long, pointed shape.

Use a skewer to serrate the leaf edges and mark veins using a knife.

Apples and pears

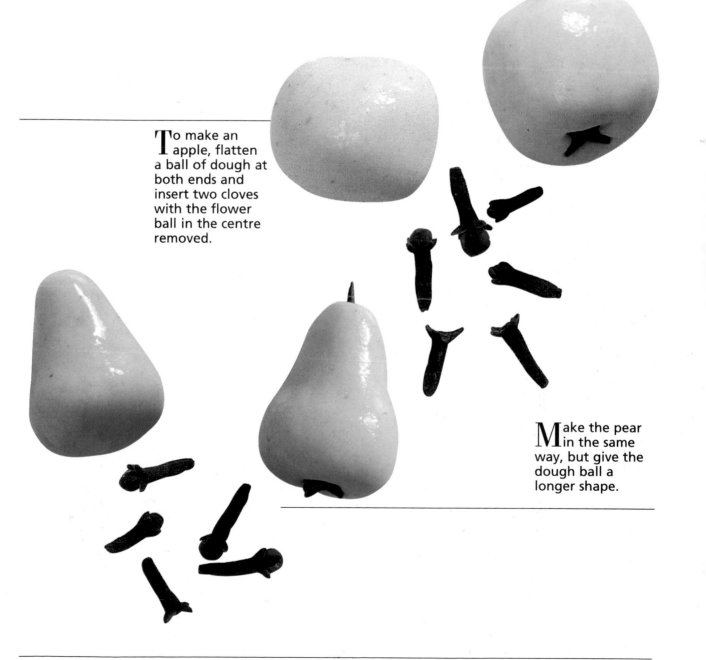

To make an apple, flatten a ball of dough at both ends and insert two cloves with the flower ball in the centre removed.

Make the pear in the same way, but give the dough ball a longer shape.

Apricots and plums

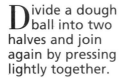**D**ivide a dough ball into two halves and join again by pressing lightly together.

Make the apricot rounder in shape than the plum, which should be more oval.

Oranges and lemons

Starting with the same ball of coloured dough as before, give the lemon its elongated shape with a character- istic bulge at the bottom, then roll the finished shape over a small grater to obtain a rough finish.

Proceed in the same way for the orange, but begin with a round shape and flatten it at both ends.

Strawberry

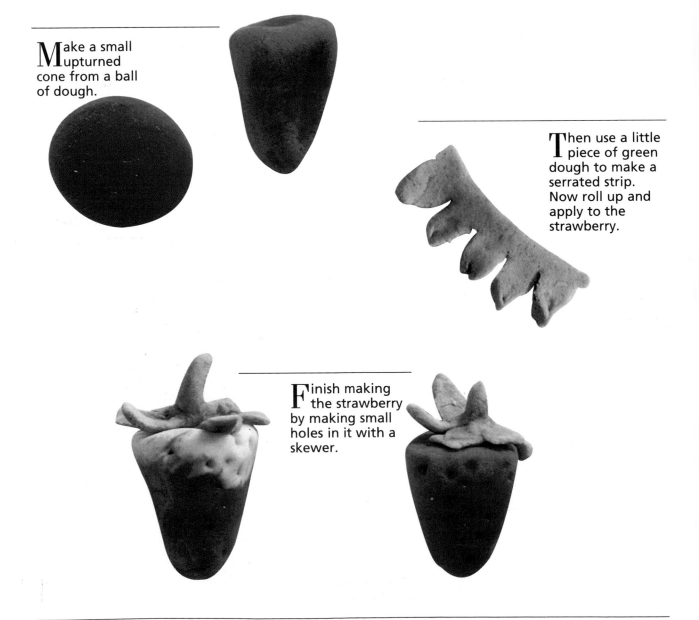

Make a small upturned cone from a ball of dough.

Then use a little piece of green dough to make a serrated strip. Now roll up and apply to the strawberry.

Finish making the strawberry by making small holes in it with a skewer.

Grape

Make dough balls of different diameters and form into a bunch.

Make a highly serrated three-lobed leaf.

Form a tendril by rolling a strip of dough in a spiral around a stick.

Assemble all the parts and add a real twig.

Blackberry or raspberry

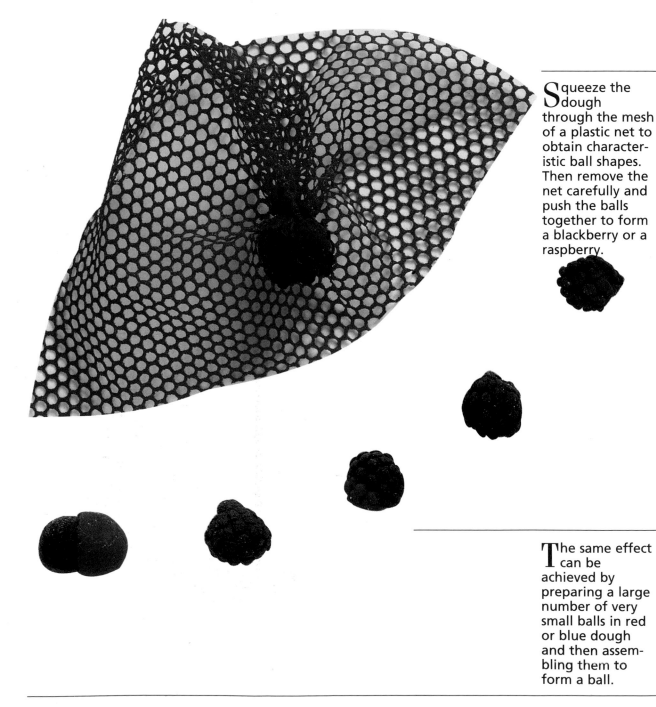

Squeeze the dough through the mesh of a plastic net to obtain characteristic ball shapes. Then remove the net carefully and push the balls together to form a blackberry or a raspberry.

The same effect can be achieved by preparing a large number of very small balls in red or blue dough and then assembling them to form a ball.

Garlic

Make deep cuts in a ball of natural-coloured dough to form cloves. Use a close-meshed strainer to make the garlic roots out of dark-coloured dough. Apply to the base of the garlic.

Carrot

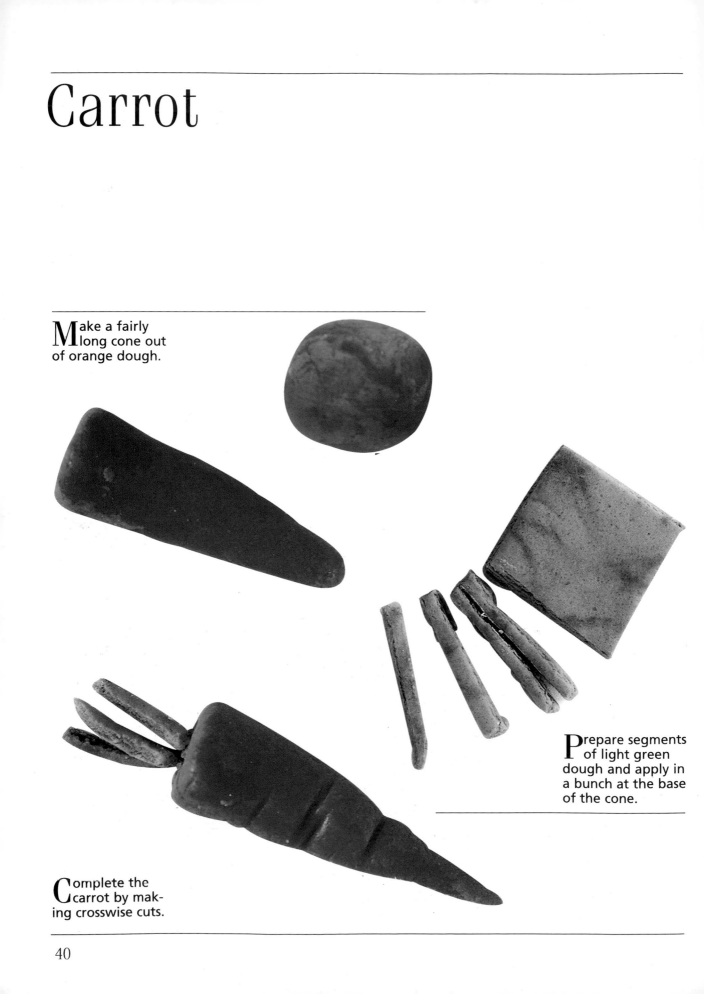

Make a fairly long cone out of orange dough.

Prepare segments of light green dough and apply in a bunch at the base of the cone.

Complete the carrot by making crosswise cuts.

Lettuce

Make the lettuce heart using natural-coloured dough.

Press light green balls against the work surface to obtain broad leaves to be wrapped around the central part.

Complete the lettuce by making other leaves in darker shades of green.

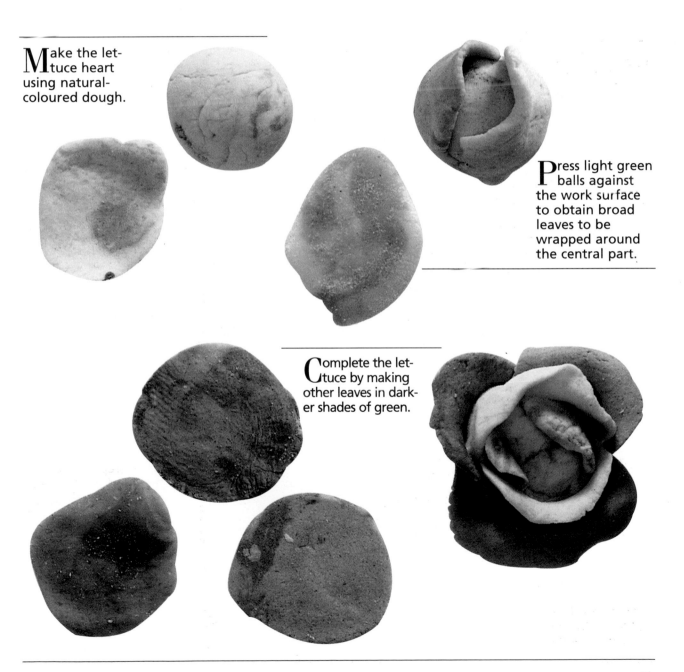

Peas

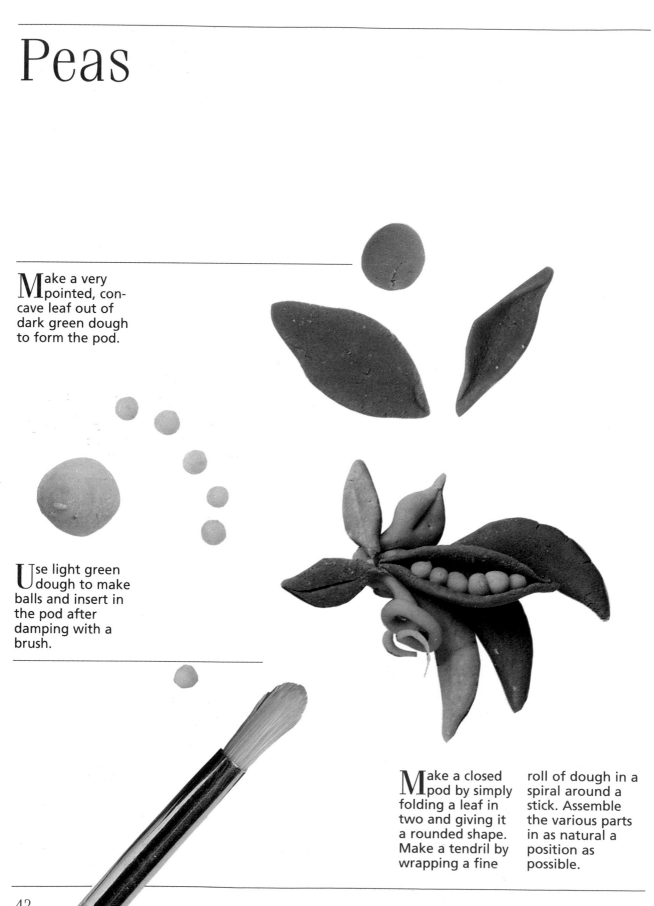

Make a very pointed, concave leaf out of dark green dough to form the pod.

Use light green dough to make balls and insert in the pod after damping with a brush.

Make a closed pod by simply folding a leaf in two and giving it a rounded shape. Make a tendril by wrapping a fine roll of dough in a spiral around a stick. Assemble the various parts in as natural a position as possible.

Pepper

Make a cylinder with rounded ends out of a ball of dough.

Press a stick lengthways against the dough to create depressions.

Remove the stalk from a red chilli pepper and push onto your red or yellow pepper.

Daffodil

Prepare balls of yellow dough. Press against the work surface to obtain long, slightly convex petals.

Overlap to form a ring of petals.

Then use orange dough to form a small trumpet with uneven edges and place in the centre of the flower.

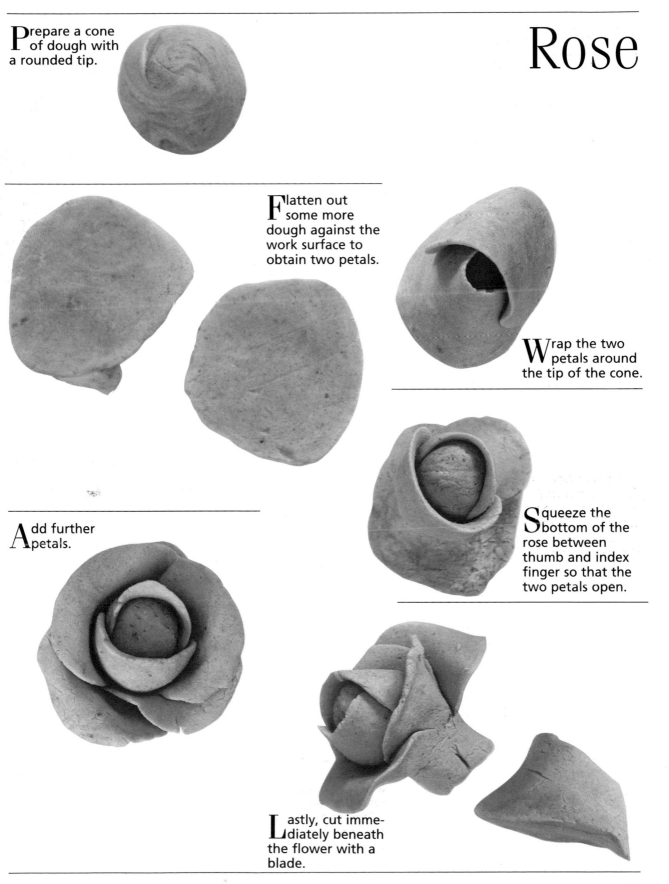

Prepare a cone of dough with a rounded tip.

Rose

Flatten out some more dough against the work surface to obtain two petals.

Wrap the two petals around the tip of the cone.

Add further petals.

Squeeze the bottom of the rose between thumb and index finger so that the two petals open.

Lastly, cut immediately beneath the flower with a blade.

45

Name plates

This plate is obtained by pressing the lid of an unusually shaped tin into a small sheet of natural-coloured dough.

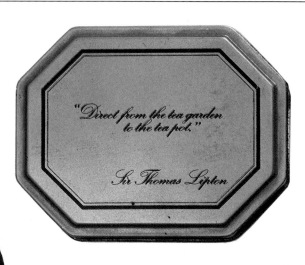

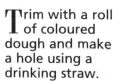

Trim with a roll of coloured dough and make a hole using a drinking straw.

Wreath

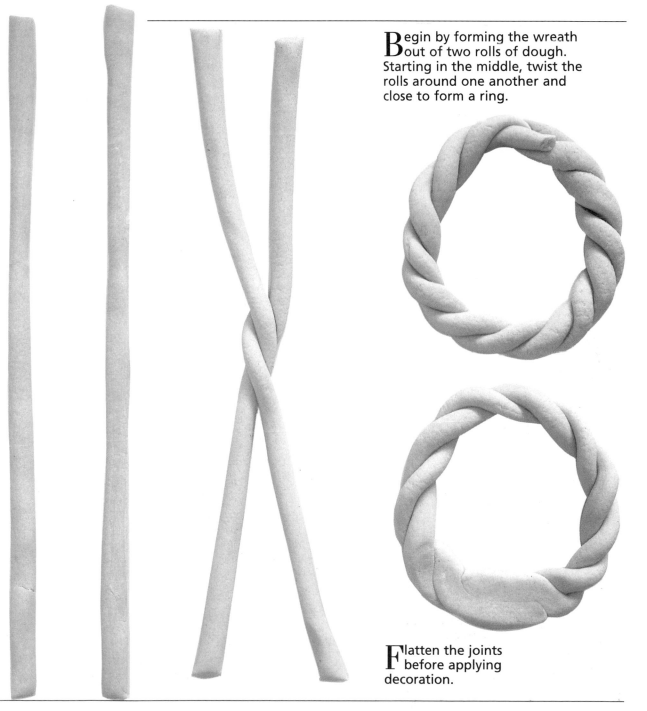

B egin by forming the wreath out of two rolls of dough. Starting in the middle, twist the rolls around one another and close to form a ring.

F latten the joints before applying decoration.

Oval

Perfect ovals may be obtained using the lids of cake and sweet tins. Decorate with flowers, the name of the recipient or words of greeting. Finish by adding a bow in the same shade.

Twist two dough rolls measuring about 30cm (12in) in length, to frame a slightly convex oval of dough.

Basket

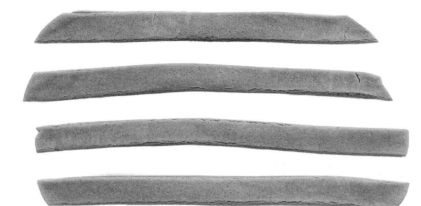

Take a sheet of biscuit-coloured dough measuring about 40cm (16in) in height, and cut strips measuring about 10cm (4in) in length. Then cut eight smaller strips measuring about 5cm (2in) in length.

Position the longer strips horizontally and the shorter strips vertically to obtain a basket-work effect.

Round off the ends and remove any excess dough. Trim the basket with dough twists.

49

Bow

Make two long, thin rectangles of dough from one ball and fold back to form loops.

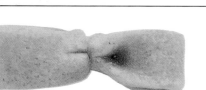

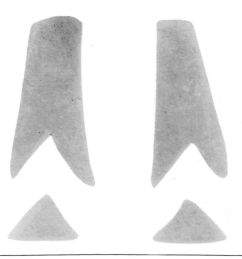

After positioning properly, finish the middle of the bow by forming a knot and two ribbons.

Teddy bear

Prepare a slightly flattened bear's body. Make arms and legs from cylinders of dough and attach to the body. Finish the head by adding muzzle, nose and ears.

Assemble all the parts with the aid of a wet paintbrush.

51

Angel

P roduce a scalloped robe and sleeves from a small sheet of dough.

M ake a cylinder of dough and curve slightly.

F ollow this sequence to assemble: first the wings and body clothed in the robe, then the arms, then the collar, and finally the head and hair.

Make a head and face, hair (use a garlic crusher) and collar.

LACE EFFECT

Begin with a small rectangle of very fine dough and produce a scalloped border using a skewer. Decorate the scalloped edge with holes and create a lace effect by printing; in this case a squashed straw was used.

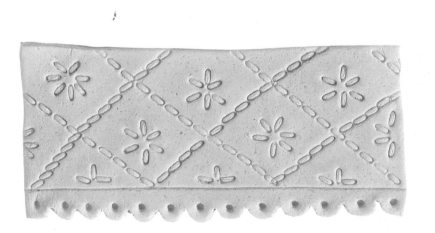

Hare

Prepare a head and two long ears beforehand and attach to the body with the aid of a toothpick. Finish with a bow.

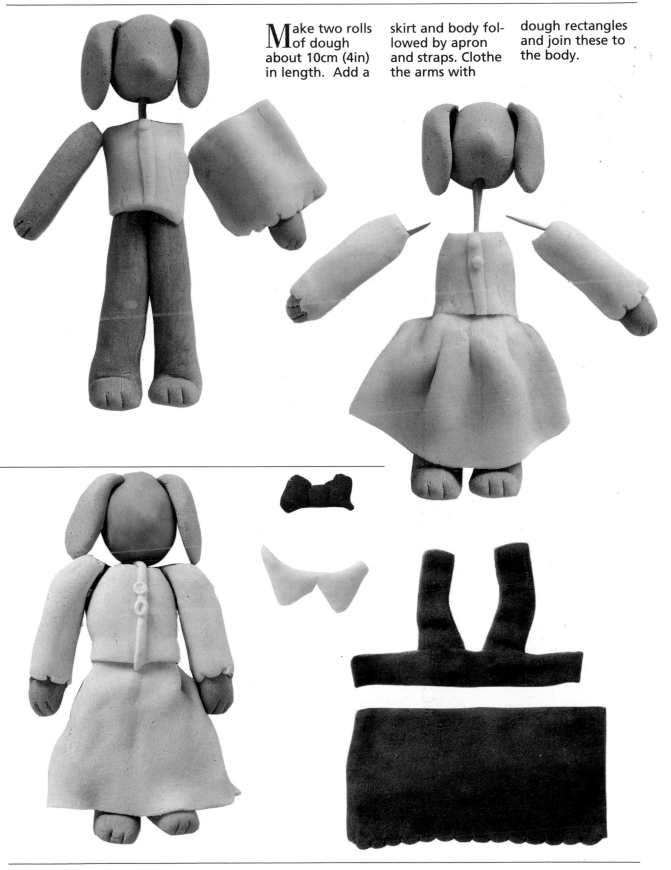

Make two rolls of dough about 10cm (4in) in length. Add a skirt and body followed by apron and straps. Clothe the arms with dough rectangles and join these to the body.

Country woman

Join two rolls of dough measuring about 10cm (4in) in length. Rest a skirt and frilled apron against the legs to cover them for three-quarters of their length and secure in place.

Add the arms clothed in scalloped dough and complete by adding a top.

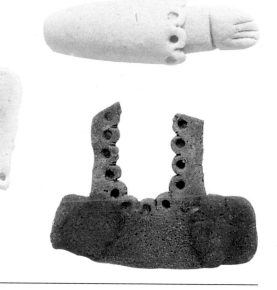

Meanwhile, make a head out of a ball of dough pushed onto a toothpick, make hair using a garlic crusher and add a headscarf. Arrange the knot to hide the point where the head is attached to the body.

GIFTS
AND IDEAS
FOR THE HOME

Wreath with small loaves

This wreath is typical of central Europe and not difficult to produce. Make a dough from 450g (14oz) each of salt and flour, and form a basic ring measuring about 8cm (31/4in) wide. Arrange small loaves, grapes, apples, pears and black peppercorns on the ring. Add gloss to parts of the wreath using egg white and leave in a medium oven for 11/2 hours to brown.

Wreath with birds

To create this wreath, which measures 23cm (91/4in) in diameter, make dough from 350g (11oz) each of salt and flour. Prepare two dough rolls, each 70cm (28in) long and 3cm (11/4in) in diameter. Twist the two rolls together and cover the join with a lace-effect heart (see page 28). Surround the heart with rosebuds, flowers decorated with cloves and two birds. Add gloss using egg-white and bake for two hours in a medium oven. Increase the heat for the last half-hour.

Heart with bow

To make this heart, which measures 25cm (10in) in height, you will need 250g (8oz) salt and 250g (8oz) flour. Prepare four rolls of dough, each measuring 45cm (18in) in length, and about 2cm (3/4in) in width, and twist to form a longish heart shape.

Wreath with spices

Use the same quantities of salt and flour (350g/11oz). This wreath is given a very distinctive appearance by adding pinches of spices such as cinnamon, paprika and curry to the natural dough to produce different shades of brown. A fine brown colour can also be obtained by adding cocoa. Cloves are extremely useful for apples and pears. The technique is as before: twist rolls of dough and add grapes, apples, pears and even roses or cherries. Because the finished composition does not require browning in an oven, simply dry at a low temperature (about 60°C/100°F) or in the open air. Finish by applying a coat of matt spray varnish.

Succulents

These simple but highly effective models are really very small. The highest only measures about 9cm (31/2in). Make the plants by placing a core of tin foil and dough inside terracotta plant pots. The plants are easily formed, using toothpicks as supports. The highly realistic spines are made using bristles from a household broom.

Summer earthenware

Rustic earthenware may be decorated with garlands of highly coloured vegetables. These are moulded directly on a cord previously glued to the earthenware. Keep a range of coloured dough at hand as you work. This will enable you to alternate, juxtapose and blend different shades and colours to create combinations to your taste. Leave to dry in the air and finish with a coat of gloss varnish.

Crown of vegetables

This crown is not easy to make but definitely worth the effort. Completely cover a 12cm (43/4in) diameter base ring with tiny vegetables. Dry in the air or the oven without exceeding 50°C (100°F). Finish with a coat of high gloss varnish.

Bowl with fruit

Model flowers and fruit in natural-coloured dough directly onto an earthenware vessel about 20cm (8in) in height. Wrap a few strands of unrefined raffia around the bowl beforehand. Dry for a long period at very low temperatures, then "wash" the decoration with very dilute paints. Pass a damp sponge over the surface of the composition to remove most of the colour and obtain a pleasing ceramic effect. Use matt spray varnish to protect the decoration. If all or part of the decoration should become detached from the bowl, replace using a spot of general purpose adhesive.

Serviette rings
with vegetables

Highly original serviette rings may be obtained by gluing a few strands of cord onto paper rings. As a final touch, mould vegetables in coloured dough directly onto the rings. Choose between cauliflowers, leeks or lettuce heads. The serviette rings may be used to indicate individual place settings.

Country dresser

This item is made entirely out of coloured dough and should be attempted only by experts. As in the case of the cabinets on pages 74 and 140, first make a box from dough about 1cm (1/2in) deep. Make the shelves by coating sturdy card in dough. The bottom part of the dresser, to which the doors are attached, is made in the same way. The goose and cloth add the final touch. The dresser, measuring 19cm (71/2in) high and 10.5cm (41/4in) wide, may be hung by inserting hooks on the back.

Great care has been taken to model the vessels, basket and flowers in this piece. Attention to detail is the most eye-catching aspect.

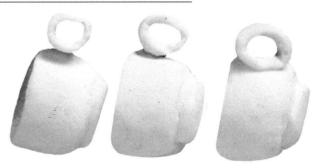

The extremely fine soup tureen and plates measure 2cm (3/4in) high, while the cups measure just 1cm (1/2in).

Toy cupboard

This highly elaborate creation calls for great patience and lots of time. It is therefore only recommended to those who have already acquired a certain level of skill. It is similar to the blue dresser on page 140 but is smaller in size. Its measurements are 19cm (71/2in) high and 18cm (71/4in) wide. Because the piece is so complex, the parts must be added one by one. Begin by preparing a sheet measuring about 1cm (1/2in) in width out of blue-coloured dough. Use this to cut out the base and side walls of the cupboard, which are assembled by damping the edges with a brush beforehand. Then fit three shelves inside the cupboard, two of which should be covered with lace made from white dough.

The half-open drawer in the lower part of the cupboard is a real test of skill. It is actually made by covering a small box with dough. Miniature toys are then arranged over the shelves, taking particular care with the dolls and their dresses. The piece is finished by adding doors previously reinforced with strong card. Treat with fixative after drying the composition in the air or in the oven at a very low temperature.

The dress is textured using a grater as explained in the section on Tricks of the Trade on page 28.

Model this doll separately as described in the Techniques section and then place inside the cupboard.

Decorated lids

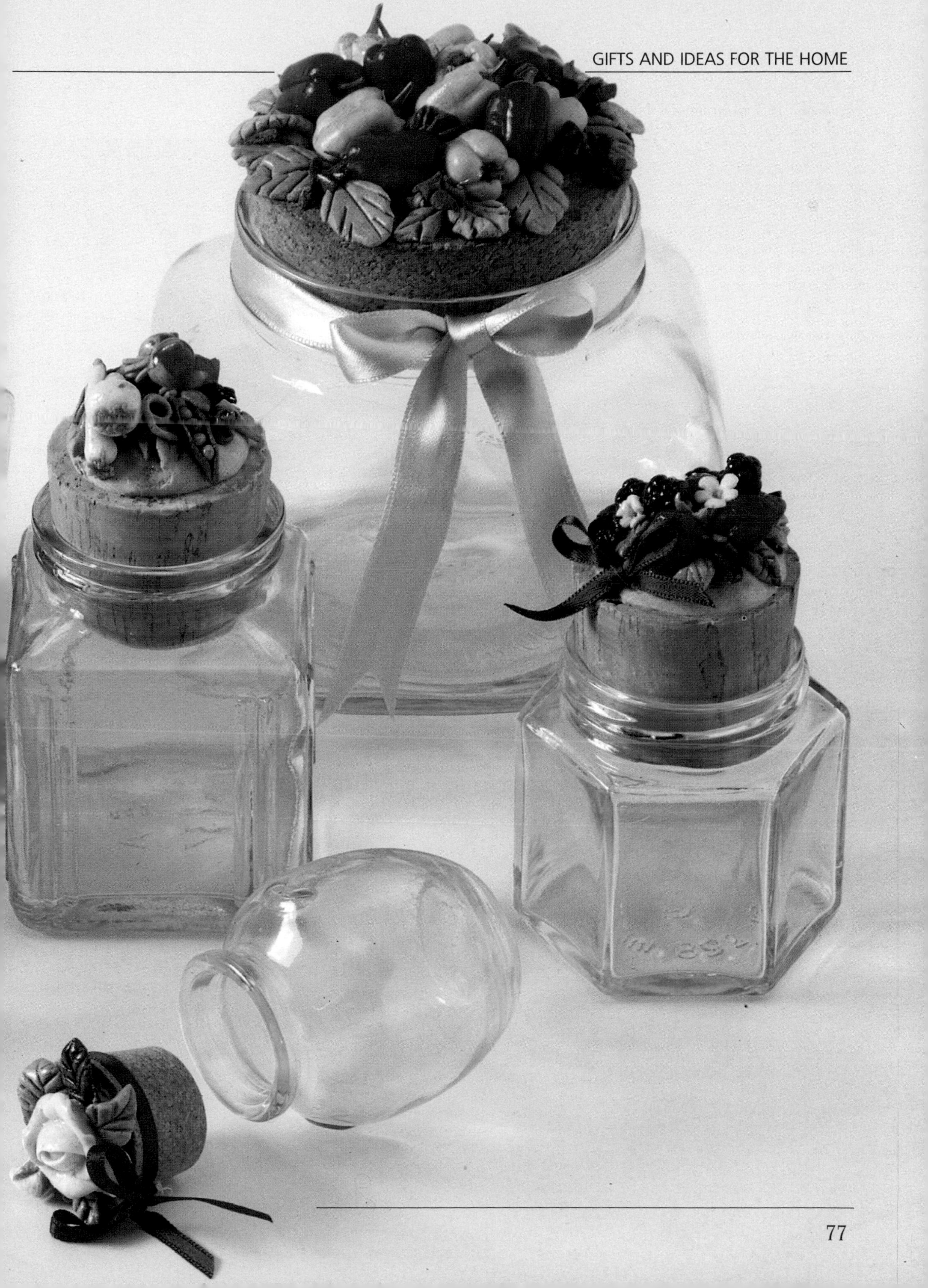

Use these cheerfully decorated cork lids to revamp the appearance of ordinary containers. The decoration is modelled and painted directly on the cork, which should be moistened slightly beforehand. Because the cork is porous, the final work will stick effectively. Do not bake but simply dry in the air. Treat with gloss varnish as a final touch.

A single rose, delicate as porcelain, is the only decoration on this lid.

Peppers are arranged on this cork lid, apparently at random, and framed by leaves in two shades of green.

These sweets are made by wrapping up a roll of dough in a very fine, coloured dough rectangle. Twist the ends of the rectangles slightly to obtain a frill.
Finish the composition by adding real sugared almonds.

This lid is decorated with a bouquet made up of many small flowers in delicate shades.

Garden and woodland themes alternate on this set of lids. The first is decorated with tiny coloured vegetables (radishes, onions and peas).

The second exploits the contrast between the red of the strawberry and the intense black of the blackberry. The work is finished with high gloss varnish.

This lid is adorned with a collection of fruit: apples, pears, strawberries and apricots. The overall effect is highlighted by a high gloss varnish.

This garlic container may be put in pride of place on a kitchen shelf.

Picture frames

Picture frames are not particularly difficult to make but are always welcome gifts. Remember to moisten the dough plait slightly when placing on the frame. Although dough sticks very effectively to untreated wood frames, part of your creation may eventually come unstuck. This problem can be overcome by using general purpose adhesive.

Frames may be dried in the air or baked slowly in an oven provided the temperature does not exceed 50°C (100°F). Pick out the decorative detail using gloss paint.

Slightly flatten the rolls of dough used for this picture frame, and make grooves along their length. Grapes and rose-buds in pastel shades are set off by the natural colour of the background.

Posies of prim-roses add a sunny touch to this cheerful white and yellow frame.

Pretty bunches of forget-me-nots stand out at opposite corners of this small, light-coloured frame.

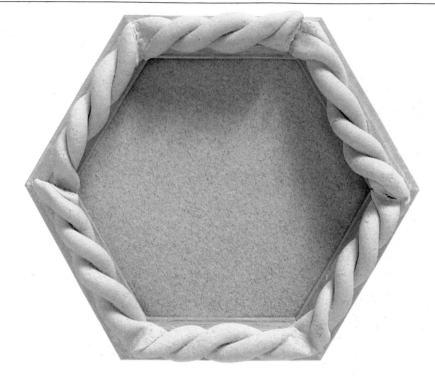

This hexagonal frame is decorated solely with blue twists of dough arranged around the edge.

The rhythm of this frame in natural dough is broken by a bow and three hearts.

A bunch of grapes adorns this pretty, pale pink picture frame.

G roove the rolls using a knife and make a two-stranded twist to form this frame. A two-toned effect is achieved by using twists of different colours.

Wall-hanging basket

This basket measures only 9cm (31/2in) in height and is modelled with great attention to detail. First make the basket following the instructions given on page 49. Then prepare a convex base from green dough, and cover with fruit, flowers and leaves. Complete the basket using matt fixative.

Box with bouquet

Improve the appearance of a dilapidated old wooden box with little expense and effort. Firstly glue on some lace "aged" in tea and use this as a base for roses in very delicate colours and leaves in two shades of green. The bouquet is completed by adding a green ribbon bow. Leave to dry in the air.

Teddy bear alphabet

This alphabet illustrates how infinite variety can be achieved beginning with one basic teddy bear shape (see page 51). Simply change the position of the bear's arms and legs to fit the letter. The letters are 8cm (31/4in) high and produced by twisting rolls of natural dough as before. The teddy bears are made from dough coloured with a little brown paint and cocoa powder and finished with matt varnish. These letters may be hung up on a wall or glued onto a frame to make a name or even the whole alphabet.

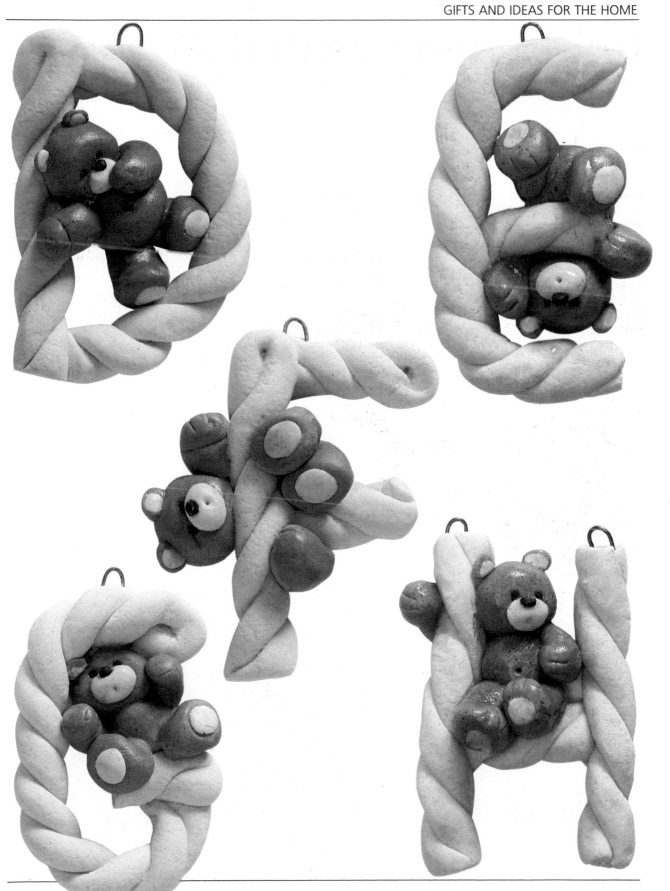

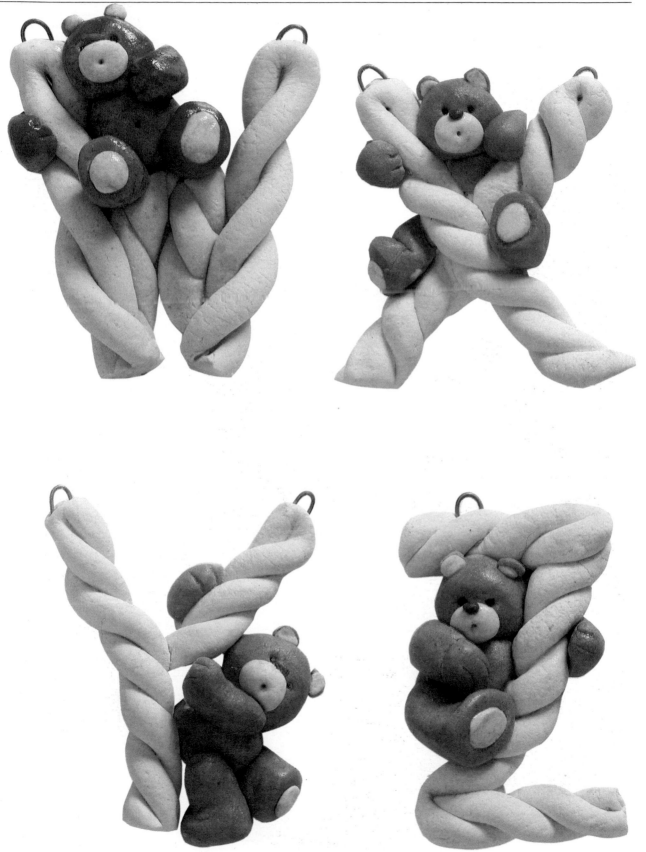

Basket with fruit

This creation is supported inside by a core of aluminium foil and made using dough coloured with spices. It is dried in an oven without exceeding 75°C (150°F) and completed with a light blue bow. The proportions are small: the basket measures only 7cm (23/4in) at its highest point.

Boxes with twists

These very similar boxes are extremely easy to make. Only the colour of the bow changes. They are modelled directly onto the card from which the box is made.

IDEAS FOR CELEBRATIONS

Heart for Mother's Day

This heart is the same size as the heart in natural dough shown on page 62. This piece features a wealth of detail and is made entirely out of dough coloured beforehand and protected by matt varnish.

Blue heart

This could be a different way to celebrate the birth of a baby boy or, in pink, would make a welcome gift for Mother's Day. First model a heart in natural coloured dough onto glass and then cover completely with small blue flowers. Dry in the open air and finish with matt varnish. Then glue a frill of lace around the entire creation.

Plaques

Follow the instructions on page 48 to form an oval, which is then framed with coloured twists or plaits. The wording is obtained by modelling dough rolls that are applied to the oval with the aid of a toothpick.

These plaques never measure more than 7cm (23/4in) in width or 5cm (2in) in height. They may be put to a thousand uses: as a gift to accompany sugared almonds at weddings, to adorn a gift package or to hang on a baby's crib. This is also a thoughtful way to remember a particular day or send greetings. The delicate appearance is underscored by flowers and bows in pastel shades.

Plaque with angels

These two plaques in natural-coloured dough look like small ivory sculptures. The oval plaque measures 16cm (63/8in) in height, whereas the round one measures 14cm (51/2in). The oval background looks different because it has been deliberately modelled in dough made with coarse salt. Plaques make a good first Communion gift and are particularly suitable for a child's bedroom.

Decorated boxes

A decorated box would form the ideal container for a small gift or some sweets. Begin by modelling the dough directly on the cover. Secure the ribbon in place. Let your imagination run free to build up a fantastic collection of boxes.

This striking composition with pink and white tulips looks, at first glance, quite difficult to make. In fact the tulips can be made easily using the end of a pencil.

Sweet containers for a baby

Make an amusing expression on the baby's face and make the model in soft colours.

This set of youthful, unusual sweet containers can be made to celebrate the birth of a baby. They are all modelled in coloured dough and finished with gloss varnish. Make the teddy bears by following the instructions on page 51 and simply adding a pink or blue gown.

Moulds and almond bags

Charming little gifts can be made using biscuit moulds. Pick out miniature flowers and fruit with gloss varnish. These may be used as place markers, package seals or as an original gift in their own right.

The beauty of this creation is its simplicity. A flower glued onto a bow creates a highly effective and delicate bag for sugared almonds.

Bride and groom plaque

This plaque may be used for celebratory or other purposes and measures 20cm (8in) in height. Use dough coloured previously. You may write a date and the couple's names on the ribbon at the bottom.

IDEAS FOR CHRISTMAS

Christmas tree decorations

Highly effective decorations can be achieved using ordinary biscuit moulds. Cut hearts, stars and small shapes out of a sheet of dough measuring 1cm (1/2in) thick. Carefully form rolls of red and green coloured dough and apply round the outside of the moulds.

Make a hole using a straw before finishing with simple Christmas motifs: leaves, small red berries or candles.

Christmas
angels

Follow the instructions on page 52 to make these Christmas angels measuring 7cm (2³/4in) in height. Use previously coloured dough to make the garland and tree, but model the angels out of natural-coloured dough. The face and hair are then finished with soft, delicate colours.

Nativity scene

After grooving two rolls of dough using a blade or dough cutter, make dough twists. Use the characters to cover the join, then paint in delicate shades before applying gloss varnish.

Crib

This original nativity scene is inspired by a terracotta crib and its simplicity is only apparent. After making a very smooth dough in natural colour, model each character with great care and then paint in soft shades. Each figure is broad-based for greater stability. Achieve this by cutting off the base after modelling the piece. The outer metal structure is made out of a fine sheet of brass, which also lights the crib. Bend the ends around the base rectangle in order to hold the upper curved strip in place. The inevitable shooting star is held in place by two metal plates.

Basket with berries

This basket (base measurement about 10cm/4in) is filled with easily-made red berries and leaves in two shades of green. A red bow and heart add the finishing touches to the composition. The work is dried in the air and varnished to provide gloss.

Wreath with fruit

T his dense wreath of leaves and fruit conjures up a Renaissance flavour. Make out of natural dough dried in the oven at a very low temperature, then colour and treat in the same way as the bowl on page 69.

Green box

The teddy bear decorating this lid is modelled entirely in coloured dough and measures about 11cm (43/4in) in height. The fur edging and pom-pom are made with the aid of a strainer. Gold threads and small balls have been added to the wreath, which is made from tiny leaves.

Drummer bear

This drummer bear is made entirely from coloured dough, except for the boots and drum. It measures about 8cm (3 1/4in) in height. Attach amusing real details such as the match-drumsticks, ball buttons and plume while the dough is still soft. A red ribbon makes this bear a welcome gift for Christmas.

Wreath with rosehips

This wreath is adorned with natural elements such as twigs and heads of rye. It has been given a Christmas flavour by applying rosehips made from red dough.

Wreath with fruit

Apply highly coloured fruit to a wreath of natural dough for a celebratory appearance.

Table centrepiece and place-settings

You will need a rigid base, preferably in metal, three very low candle holders and golden beads to make this centrepiece.

Although not very difficult to make, this creation is time-consuming but bound to be a success. Firstly position the candle holders on a fine metal base and then add a considerable number of fruits and flowers modelled in coloured dough directly onto the base. Secure to the base. The party flavour is highlighted by scattering small balls and sugared almonds here and there together with heads of wild rye. Place a fruit and flowers in the middle of a base consisting of three leaves and add a white heart with the guest's name written on it to obtain beautiful place-settings. Choose candle colours to blend in with the main colour of the composition to add a further touch of style.

Father Christmas

This original Father Christmas is all in white with a jute sack and gifts. Make out of coloured dough and form the fur edging using a strainer.

Dressing the tree

Daddy bear and baby bear are decorating this beautiful Christmas tree. Model out of coloured dough by lying branches on top of one another and working from the bottom. Complete the effect by adding baubles and candles in coloured dough.

Grandfather clock

This grandfather clock is cut out of a sheet of dough measuring about 5mm (1/4in) thick Made from coloured dough, it measures just 10cm (4in) high and is decorated with a bow and holly branch.

Made from dough coloured with cocoa powder, this dresser is about 10cm (4in) high and is decorated with a charming Christmas tree.

Bear at the window

Firstly model the window frame on a small blue sheet, then add the wreath and snowflakes. Lastly, fix the bear carefully onto the window.

Sleeping bear

The trick in this piece is to produce a three-dimensional effect even though the piece is only a few centimetres deep. Mark squares on the quilt using a blade, then fit the quilt onto the bed and decorate with dots for a very effective result.

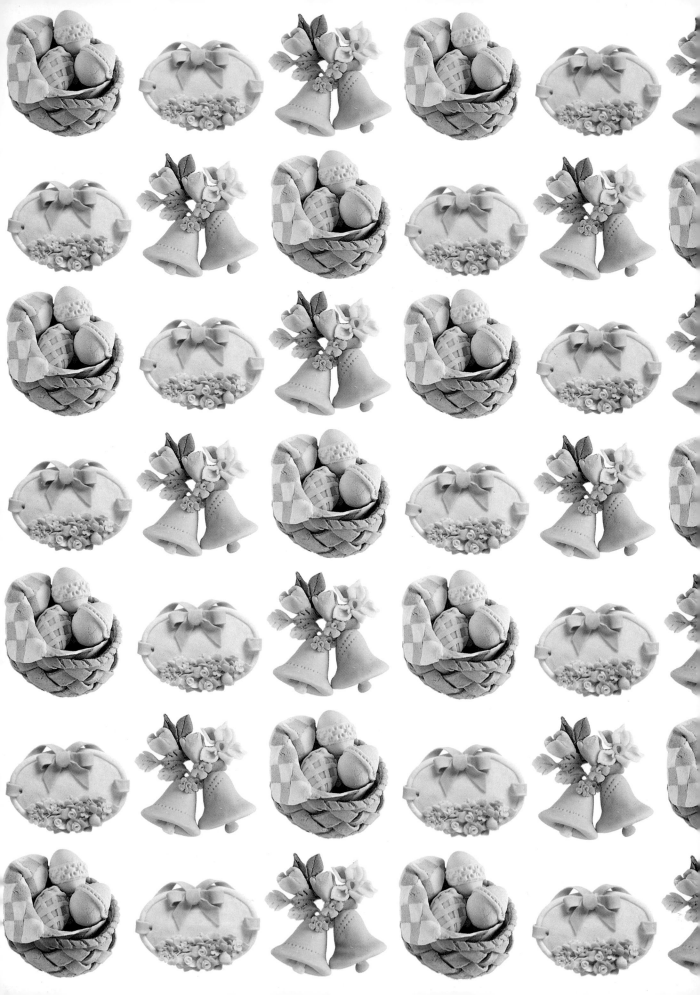

IDEAS FOR EASTER

Plaques and basket with chickens

These two medallions are easy to make and represent an unusual way to send Easter greetings. They may also be used as place-markers or to send affectionate greetings.

First make a basket using biscuit-coloured dough strips, then fill with chickens. Make these by joining two balls of yellow dough and applying small wings and an orange beak.

Bells

Colour is the main feature of this dough model. The piece is easy to make and the bells help to create a festive atmosphere.

Ideas with eggs

This festive spring-like wreath measures 9cm (31/2in) in diameter. Minute details such as the tiny flowers, eggs and bows are the main feature of this work.

These cheerfully coloured eggs are very easy to make. Small forget-me-nots add a charming touch to each egg.

Weave strands of dough together to form a basket on a round base as explained on page 49. Use previously coloured dough to make a cloth onto which clear white eggs are placed.

Blue dresser

This dresser is exactly the same as the toy cupboard on page 74. Easter eggs, china and egg baskets make a fine show inside, while linen tumbles out of the drawer. The whole piece measures 22cm (9in) in height and 24cm (91/2in) in width, including the two open doors. The entire piece is made from coloured dough.

The flowers, basket and wreath may be used as starting points for much larger works.

Make the decorations on plates and cups out of coloured dough so you do not need to paint the finished work.

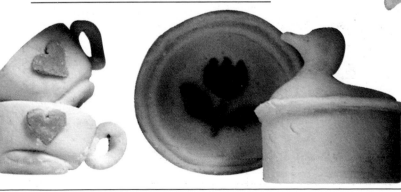

Spring basket

Weave the dough to form a strip and fasten to a round base. Place aluminium foil inside the basket and fill with green coloured dough. Complete the composition with tiny flowers in pastel colours. The entire piece measures only about 6cm (23/8in) in height.

CHARACTERS

Country cousins

These bread figures represent country characters caught in the middle of their day-to-day activities: men gathering fruit and vegetables, and women knitting or tending farm animals. The figures are first modelled in coloured dough and then painted. Surprising effects can be achieved. The figures seem to be wearing real garments made from flowered or checked cotton. Finish with gloss varnish. The figures measure no more than 10cm (4in) in height.

The cheeks of this plump-faced farmer are as red as the apples in his basket.

Make this country woman with scarf by following the instructions on page 32. Note the minutely decorated plate.

Gloss varnish makes the children with basket and doll shown alongside look as if they are made from porcelain.

This knitting grandma is seated on a cube of dough. Extra interest is added by certain real details, namely metal spectacles, balls of wool and knitting.

Here is a farmer returning from the fields with cabbages and lettuces. His wheelbarrow is supported inside by toothpicks.

This farmer looks as if he is posing for a photograph with his dog. The spade handle is made out of a toothpick.

The shirt of this farmer holding grapes is painted in great detail using a fine brush.

These two farmers' wives struggling with their geese are very similar. Both wear lacy aprons, knotted scarves and sprigged cotton. Follow the instructions on page 21-22.

Hares

Following the instructions on page 54 you can create an infinite number of variations on the same theme, as with these hares. The important thing is to devote great attention to detail. These hares measure up to 15cm (6in) in height. Here we see a mother and daughter hare carrying gifts.

This hare's striped dress is very effective. It is carefully painted to look like real fabric.

This baby's suit is so skilfully made that it appears to be warm and soft. The mother's dress is time-consuming to make and based on Provençal prints.

Because the seated position of this hare poses problems, the figure is supported by using stiff material. The decoration on the suit is very imaginative.

Here is our hare dressed in his Sunday best. What could be more fun than celebrating a birthday?

The two bears

These bears are fun to make as well. Measuring 5-10cm (2-4in) in height, they are a variation on the basic model described on page 51. Here we see two friends embracing.

Bear kneading dough

Dough, the theme of this manual, also provides the subject for our last picture: a mother and daughter contentedly kneading on a sturdy table.

Table of difficulty

Wreath with small loaves	★★	Box with bouquet		
Wreath with birds	★★	Teddy bear alphabet	★	
Heart with bow	★★	Basket with fruit	★	
Wreath with spices	★★	Boxes with twists		
Succulents	★	Heart for Mother's Day	★	
Summer earthenware	★★★	Blue heart	★	
Crown of vegetables	★★★	Plaques	★	
Bowl with fruit	★★	Plaque with angels	★	
Serviette rings with vegetables	★★	Decorated boxes		
Country dresser	★★★	Sweet containers for a baby	★	
Toy cupboard	★★★	Moulds and bags for		
Decorated lids	★★	sugared almonds		★
Picture frames	★★	Medallions with bride and groom	★★	
Wall-hanging basket	★★	Christmas tree decorations		★

Easy	★		
Moderately difficult	★★		
For experts	★★★		

Christmas angels	★★	Bear at the window	
Nativity scene	★★	Sleeping bear	★
Crib	★★★	Plaques for Easter	
Basket with berries	★	Basket with chickens	
Wreath with fruit	★★	Bells	
Green box	★★	Ideas with eggs	
Drummer bear	★★	Blue dresser	★
Wreath with rose-hips	★	Spring basket	
Wreath with fruit	★	Country cousins	
Table centrepiece and place-settings	★★	Hares	★
Father Christmas	★★	The two bears	★
Dressing the tree	★★	Bear kneading dough	★
Grandfather clock	★		
Dresser	★★		

Index